ALL EARS!
Scan this QR code on your smartphone or tablet for a free audio reading of this book!

Scan the code, hear the story!

Having trouble?
Visit www.hpgentileschi.com
for help!

For Isabella, Madelyn & Quinn,
who we love to make (and EAT)
ice-cream with.

H.P. Gentileschi Publishing House
Austin - Rome

www.hpgentileschi.com

I see an *iguana* in my ice-cream!

I see ice-creams in Italy !

Short Ĭ Words

insects

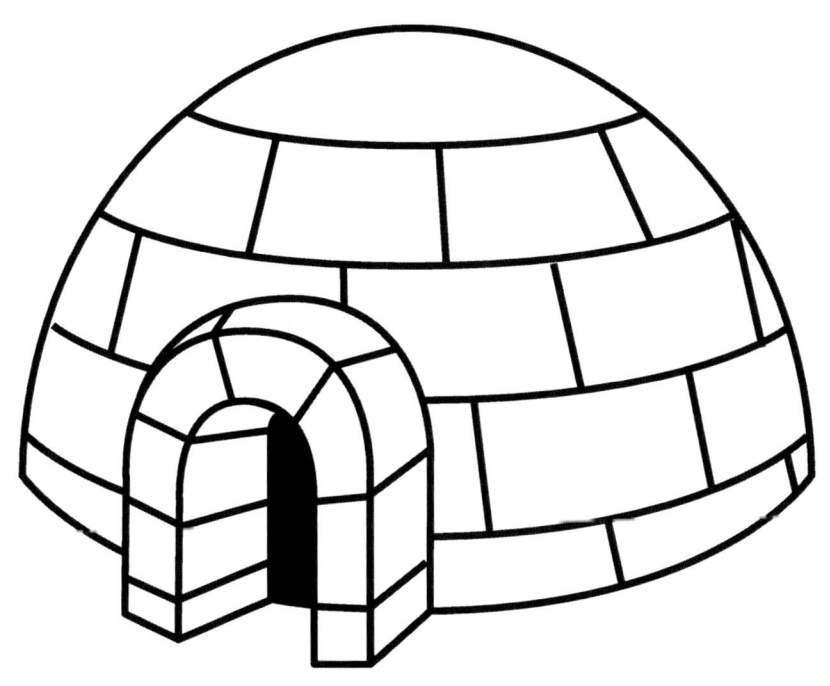

igloo

invitation

iguana

Long Ī Words

ice-cream

ivy

iron

ice-skate

island

icing

I is for digital INK and photos in Italy!

To make these illustrations, digital INK was used to draw cartoons onto ice-cream photos taken in Italy.

MAKE YOUR OWN
INK on a digital photo art!

1. Take a photo of an ice-cream with your phone or tablet.

2. Print it in color on white copy paper.

3. Use an ink marker to draw an object that starts with the letter I.

I

This book's LETTER ACTION

Hold one hand like you are holding an empty ice cream cone and use the other to place an ice cream scoop IN it, and say: "i, i, in"

UDL and H.P. Gentileschi

At H.P. Gentileschi Publishing House, we create all our books and resources using the Universal Design for Learning (UDL) inclusive principle. The goal of UDL is to provide multiple means of teaching methods and materials to remove any barriers to learning and give all children equal opportunities to grow.

For this reason, you will find our books in numerous media forms:
- In print on paperback with easy-to-read fonts and not overly busy illustrations
- Digital eBooks on Amazon Kindle
- Audiobooks linked to each book with QR codes

Our books also come with fun experiential learning activities, such as Letter Actions and craft projects that provide physical movement options that reinforce the book's teaching objectives.

These UDL resources can be helpful for all kids, including English Language Learners and kids with diverse learning and attention abilities. Our book and curriculum characters represent the beautiful diversity that is found in our world, so every child feels included.

AlphaBOX Book Series

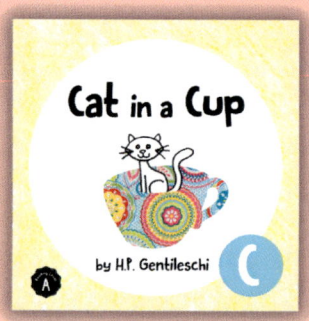

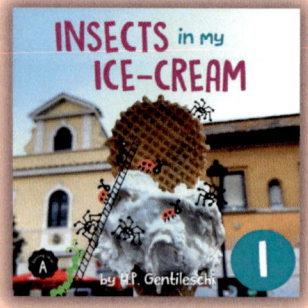

  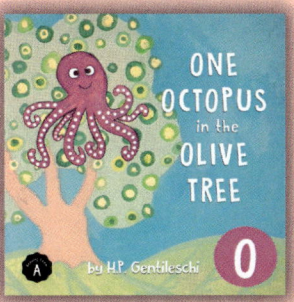 
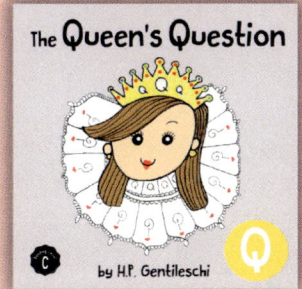  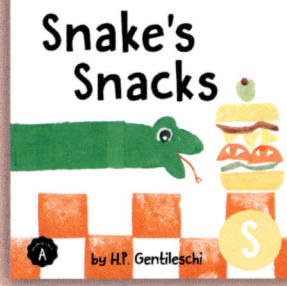 
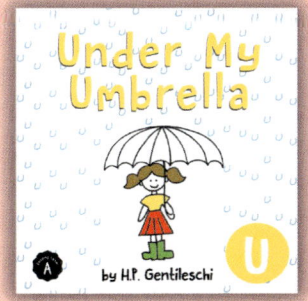   

H.P. Gentileschi
Publishing House
www.HPgentileschi.com

For all of our Letter Name actions, visit our website!
www.hpgentileschi.com

2023 © H.P. Gentileschi Publishing House LLC. All rights reserved. No part of this publication may be reproduced, stored in a retrieval system, or transmitted in any form or by any means, electronic, mechanical, photocopying, recording, or otherwise without the prior permission of the publisher.

The name H.P. Gentileschi and the device are Trade Marks of H.P. Gentileschi Publishing House LLC.

Educators and librarians, for a variety of teaching tools, visit www.hpgentileschi.com

Printed in the U.S.A.

For more engaging activities, teaching resources and to learn more about AlphaBOX books, follow H.P. Gentileschi Publishing House on:

www.hpgentileschi.com

We'd love to see how you're using the AlphaBOX series!

Share and tag your photos using:
#alphaboxbooks

Made in the USA
Middletown, DE
06 December 2024

66277583R00020